Humble, Happy & Wise

Selected Stories from *Living with the Himalayan Masters*

by Swami Rama

Also by Swami Rama

The Royal Path: Practical Lessons on Yoga
A Practical Guide to Holistic Health
Celestial Song/Gobind Geet
Choosing a Path
Exercises for Joints and Glands
Fearless Living: Yoga and Faith
Happiness Is Your Creation
Living with the Himalayan Masters
Love and Family Life
Love Whispers
Meditation and Its Practice
Path of Fire and Light
Path of Fire and Light, Volume 2
Perennial Psychology of the Bhagavad Gita
Science of Breath
Spirituality: Transformation Within & Without
Swami Rama Gift Book Set
The Art of Joyful Living
The Royal Path: Practical Lessons on Yoga
Yoga and Psychotherapy

Humble, Happy & Wise

Collected Stories by

SWAMI RAMA

www.HimalayanInstitute.in

Himalayan Institute India
A-43, Second Floor, Sector 7
Noida-201301 (U.P.) India
Phone: 0120-4247856/57
Email: hipress@himalayaninstitute.in

www.HimalayanInstitute.in

Cover design by Cheri Knuth
Creative direction and design by Cheri Knuth

The paper used in this publication meets the minimum requirements of American National Standard for Information Sciences–Permanence of Paper for printed Library Materials, ANSI Z39.48-1984.

Library of Congress Cataloging-in-Publication Data

Rama, Swami
Humble, Happy & Wise
ISBN: 0-89389-230-0
1.Yoga. I. Title

To cultivate the quality of humility

is one step toward enlightenment.

By being humble we gain much and lose nothing.

Prayer and contemplation strengthen our willpower

in cultivating this inner quality.

About the Swami Rama Book Series

Yogi, spiritual adept, teacher, author, and founder of the Himalayan Institute, Swami Rama brought health, peace and happiness to the lives of tens of thousands. The essence of his profound yet simple teachings continues to inspire and direct the lives of sincere seekers around the world. *Freedom From Fear* is a selection of stories from his classic work, *Living With the Himalayan Masters.*

Table of Contents

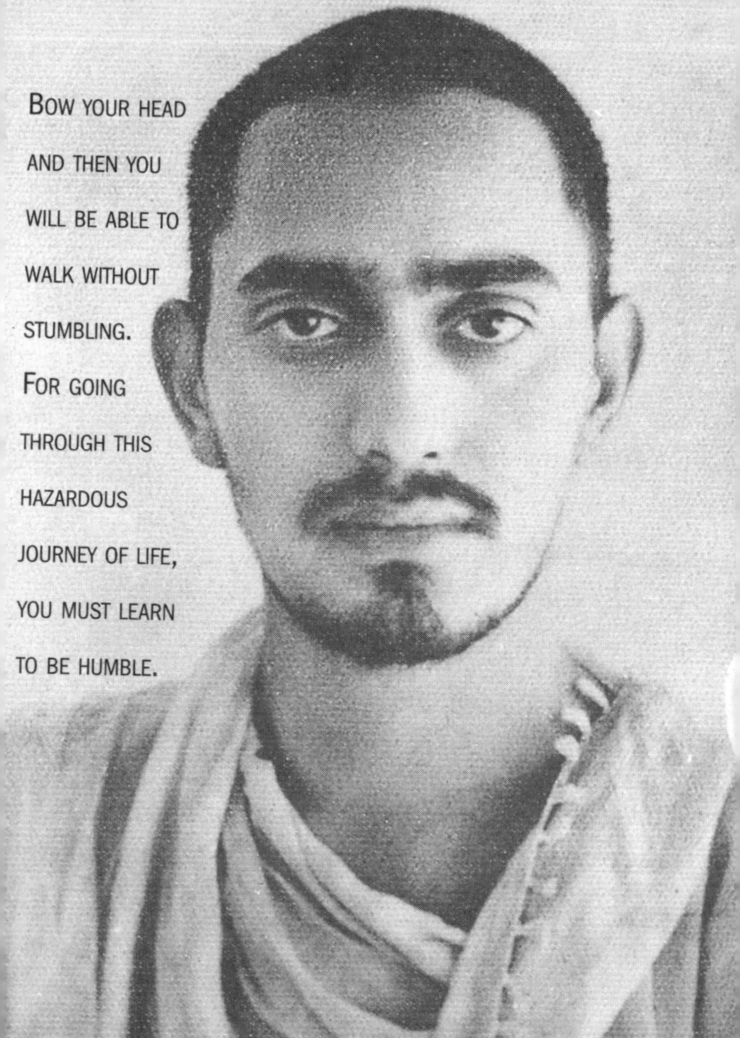
BOW YOUR HEAD
AND THEN YOU
WILL BE ABLE TO
WALK WITHOUT
STUMBLING.
FOR GOING
THROUGH THIS
HAZARDOUS
JOURNEY OF LIFE,
YOU MUST LEARN
TO BE HUMBLE.

Ego and Vanity Are in Vain

Once my master lived in a holy place of the Himalayas called Tungnath. On the way to see him I stopped at Karnaprayag, a shrine in the mountains. A renowned swami, Prabhat Swami, lived in a cave near the shrine, so I went to visit him. He was seated on a blanket which had been folded into quarters, and a few villagers were seated before him. I greeted him according to our tradition. I expected him to offer me a seat beside him. I was being trained to be a swami at that time, and I was still suffering from an inflated ego, at least partly because people in the villages of India respect all swamis and bow down to them. This feeds the ego and creates many problems for a swami in training. Prabhat Swami knew my problem. He smiled and said, "Please take your seat."

I asked, "Could you please unfold your blanket so I can sit next to you?" I insisted, but he just laughed at me. I asked, "Why won't you let me sit next to you?" I was quite conceited and impolite.

He quoted the dialogue between Rama and Hanuman in the Yoga Vasishtha, saying, "'Eternally we are one and the same, but as human beings, you are still a servant and I am your master.'

Modern man tries to have the position of a master without attaining anything."

Then he gave me a lesson, saying, "A man went to see a master who was seated on a high platform teaching many people. The man held a distinguished position in society, so he chafed at being treated like all the rest of the students, without getting special attention. He went up to the master and asked, 'Sir, can I sit on the same platform with you?'

"The master said, 'You should know the role of a student as well as the role of a master.'

"The man asked, 'Sir, what are the duties of a student?'

"The master explained, 'A student cleans, serves, washes dishes, cooks food, prepares and purifies himself, and serves his master.'

"Then the man asked, 'And what does a master do, sir?'

"'A master teaches–he doesn't do any of the menial work.'

"'Why can't I become a master without doing all of

this?' asked the man. 'The menial work has nothing to do with my learning how to teach.'

"The master said, 'No, you will be hurting yourself and hurting others. You have to understand from the very beginning that the spiritual path can tolerate everything but ego.'"

Ego places a veil between the aspirant and the process of learning. When you become egocentric you isolate yourself and are not able to communicate with your teacher or with your own conscience, and you don't follow the instructions of the teacher. Such an ego needs austerities and modifications, without which all knowledge drains away.

GO PLACES A EIL BETWEEN IE ASPIRANT ND THE ROCESS OF ARNING.

My Swollen Ego

During the rainy season swamis do not travel, but stay in one place for four months. People come to learn the scriptures from them. Although I was still being trained as a swami, I too would teach every day.

Students often create problems for a teacher. For instance, the first thing they do is place him high above them so that there is limited communication. My students built a high platform on which I was asked to sit. I was inordinately proud that I had a large following. That happens when you are a neophyte and hanker after name and fame. The more one's followers increase, the more egotistical one becomes.

The teachings of the Sages are not understood by the ordinary mind, or even by the intellectual mind. Intuitive knowledge alone leads to understanding them.

I had the impression that one particular swami among my students was not very knowledgeable. During my lectures he sat quietly in a corner. This swami was actually an advanced adept, although I was not aware of it. He had come because I prayed to the Lord, "Lord, enlighten me. Help me, Lord." I sincerely cried and prayed, so the Lord sent that man to me. And what did I do? I gave him my loincloth to wash, and all day I would order him to do things for me. He was with me for two months before he decided to teach me a lesson.

One morning we were both sitting on a rock on a bank of the Ganges. While brushing my teeth, I ordered, "Go and fetch me some water." He had had enough of my swollen ego. He said, "Go on brushing." I lost awareness of what was happening after that. Two days later someone found me lying there. My face was horribly swollen. I had dropped the brush but was still continuously rubbing my finger in my mouth. I was doing it unconsciously. My master appeared and said, "Get up!" I opened my eyes but could not lift my face, it was so heavy. My gums were swollen and I could not move my jaw.

Then my master told me, "That swami is a great sage. God sent him to you. You do not know how to be humble and behave properly with the men of God. Now I hope you have learned a lesson. Do not commit this mistake again." Then he said, "Get up; look at the sky and start walking."

I protested, "If I look at the sky and continue walking, I will stumble and fall." He said, "Bow your head and then you will be able to walk without stumbling. For going through this hazardous journey of life, you must learn to be humble. Ego and pride are two stumbling blocks on this journey. If you are not humble, you cannot learn. Your growth will be stunted."

When one begins to tread the path of spirituality it is essential to be humble. Ego creates barriers, and the faculty of discrimination is lost. If discrimination is not sharpened, reason does not function properly and there is no clarity of mind. A clouded mind is not a good instrument on the path of enlightenment.

EGO AND PRIDE ARE TWO STUMBLING BLOCKS ON THIS JOURNEY.

Intuition and Humbleness

When I was in Shrinagar, Kashmir, I met a great scholar of Vedanta who was head of the department of philosophy in a renowned university. He said, "If I can answer your questions, I will be glad to do so."

So I put these questions to him: "The Upanishads appear to be full of contradictions. In one place they say that Brahman is one without a second. Somewhere else they say that everything is Brahman. In a third place they say this world is false and Brahman alone is truth. And in a fourth place it is said that there is only one absolute Reality beneath all these diversities. How can one make sense out of these conflicting statements?"

He replied, “I don’t know how to answer a swami’s questions. You are learning to be a swami of the Shankaracharya order. You should know the answers better than I.”

I went to many other learned people, but nobody could satisfy me. They could give me commentaries on different Upanishads, but no one could resolve these apparent contradictions. Eventually I went to a swami near Uttarkashi, 135 miles deep in the Himalayas. His name was Vishnu Maharaj. He was always naked, having no clothes or any other possessions. I said to him, “I want to know something about the Upanishads.”

He said, “Bow down first. You are asking about the Upanishads with a swollen ego. How can you possibly learn these subtle truths?”

I did not like to bow down before anyone, so I left his place. After that, whenever I inquired about the Upanishads I was told, "Go to Vishnu Maharaj. No one else can answer you." But I didn't want to ask him because he knew that my whole problem was my ego, and he immediately tested me by saying, "Bow down and then I will answer your question." I wouldn't do that. I tried my best to find other swamis who could answer these questions, but everyone I asked referred me to Vishnu Maharaj.

Every day I would approach the cave where he lived on a bank of the Ganges. I would think, "Let me see how he answers my questions." But when I got near I would become very fearful of the impending confrontation, so I would change my mind and go back.

One day he saw me nearby and said, "Come, sit down. Are you hungry? Do you want to eat with me?" He was very pleasant and gracious. He gave me food and drink and then said, "Now you should go. I have no more time to spend with you today."

I said, "I have come with certain questions, sir. Food and drink I can get elsewhere. I want spiritual food." He said, "You are not prepared. In your mind you want to examine me; you want to know whether I can answer your questions or not; you don't want to learn. When you are prepared, come to me and I will answer you." The next day I became very humble and I said, "Sir, the whole night I prepared myself, and now I'm ready!"

Then he taught me, and all my questions were

resolved. Answering my questions systematically, he said that there are no contradictions in the teachings of the Upanishads. These teachings are received directly by the great sages in a deep state of contemplation and meditation.

He explained, "When the student starts practicing, he realizes that this apparent world is changeable, while truth never changes. Then he knows that the world of forms and names which is full of changes is false, and that behind it there exists an absolute Reality that is unchanging.

"In the second step, when he has known the truth, he understands that there is only one truth and that truth is omnipresent, so there is really nothing like falsehood. In that stage he knows that reality which is one and the same in both the finite and infinite worlds. But there is another, higher, state in which the aspirant realizes that there is only one absolute Reality without second, and that that which is apparently false is in reality a manifestation of the absolute One.

"These apparent contradictions confuse only that student who has not studied the Upanishads from a competent teacher. A competent teacher makes the student aware of the experiences one has on various levels. These are the levels of consciousness, and there is no contradiction in them." He continued: "The teachings of the Upanishads are not understood by the ordinary mind or even by the intellectual mind. Intuitive knowledge alone leads to understanding them."

In fact, I wanted to strengthen the knowledge which I had received from my master, and knowingly posed such questions to others. The sages never answer questions posed without humbleness. The questions are resolved by humility itself. This great man taught me to rise above intellectual arguments and instructed me to allow intuition to flow uninterruptedly to answer such subtle questions.

THE SAGES NEVER ANSWER QUESTIONS POSED WITHOUT HUMBLENESS

FROM THE EXPERIENCES THAT THESE SAGES GAVE ME I BEGAN TO REALIZE THE DIFFERENCE BETWEEN BOOK KNOWLEDGE AND EXPERIENTIAL KNOWLEDGE.

Lessons in Humility

As a young man I thought I had perfected myself and that I didn't need any further teaching or study. I felt there was no swami in India as advanced as I because I seemed to be more intellectually knowledgeable than others, and I was myself teaching many swamis. When I conveyed this inflated opinion of myself to my master, he looked at me and asked, "Are you drugged? What do you mean?" I said, "No, really. This is the way I feel."

He returned to the subject a few days later. "You are still a child. You only know how to attend college. You have not mastered four things. Master them and then you will have attained something.

"Have a desire to meet and know God. But have no

selfish desire to acquire things for yourself. Give up all anger, greed, and attachment. Practice meditation regularly. Only when you have done these four things will you become perfect."

Then he told me to visit certain sages. He said, "When you are with them you should be very humble. If you become obstinate or aggressive, you will be deprived of their knowledge. They will just close their eyes and sit in meditation." He said this because he knew that I was very obstinate and impatient.

He gave me a list of sages of different orders. They were his friends who had known me from a young age because I had been with him when he visited them. I had been quite mischievous. I used to pester them and throw things at them so that they would know I was around. Whenever they came to visit my master they would ask, "Is he still with you?"

First I went to see a swami who was renowned for silence. He had withdrawn from worldly concerns. No matter what happened around him, he never looked up.

On my way I talked with villagers nearby. They told me, "He doesn't talk to anyone or look at anyone; he doesn't even eat. This is the third month he has been in the same place without getting up. We have never seen such a man." This state is called *ajagar-vritti*, which means "python's tendency." Just as a python remains in a dormant state for a long time, some sages do not move for many days, but remain in a deep state of meditation.

When I found him he was laying on a hillock under a

banyan tree, smiling, with his eyes closed, as though he were the lord of the universe. He never wore anything, whether it was summer, winter, or the rainy season. His skin appeared weather proof, like that of an elephant. He did not own a thing, but he was utterly content.

When I first saw him lying that way, I thought, “At least he should have a little decency.” Then I thought, “My master told me to visit him, and I know that my master would not waste my time. I am only seeing his body.” I touched his feet. [According to custom, when we touch the feet of great men, they bless us.]

But he was not sensitive to external stimuli; he was somewhere else. Three or four times I said, “Hello, sir; how are you?” But he did not respond. There was no movement, no answer. Then I started massaging his feet.

I thought he would be pleased, but he kicked me. That kick was so strong that I was thrown backward all the way down the hill, which was quite steep, and into a lake below. I fell against many trees and rocks on the way down and ended up with many painful bruises.

I was vindictive. "What reason has he to do this? I came to him in reverence, massaged his feet–and he kicked me! He's not a sage. I'll teach him: I'll break both his legs! I'll give him double what he gave me!" I really wanted to retaliate. I decided that perhaps my master sent me to him to teach him a lesson.

When I returned to the hill to vent my anger, he was sitting up and smiling. He said, "How are you, son?"

I said, "How am I? After kicking me and knocking me down the hill, you're asking how I am?"

He said, “Your master told you to master four things, and you have not even mastered one. I kicked you to test your control of anger. Now you are so angry that you cannot learn anything. You are not tranquil. You are still very immature. You don’t follow the spiritual teaching of your master, who is so selfless. What could you possibly learn from me? You are not prepared for my teachings. Go away!”

Nobody had ever talked to me like that. When I thought about what he said, I realized that it was true; I was completely possessed by my anger.

He asked, “Do you know why we touch the feet of a sage?” Then he recited a beautiful Persian belief: “A sage gives the best part of his life, surrendering it at the lotus feet of the Lord. People ordinarily recognize you only by your face—but the face of the sage is not here; it is with his Lord. People find only feet here, so they bow to the feet."

He said, "You should have that humility when touching someone's feet. Now you cannot stay here. You will have to go."

I wept and thought, "A few days ago I thought I was perfect, but surely I am not." Then I said, "Sir, I will come back to you when I have really conquered my ego." And I departed.

All the kicks and blows of life teach us something. No matter whence they come, they are blessings in disguise if we learn their lesson. Buddha said, "For a wise man, there is nothing to be called bad. Any adversity of life provides a

FOR A WISE MAN, THERE IS NOTHING TO BE CALLED BAD.

step for his growth, provided he knows how to utilize it."

I visited another swami and determined that no matter what he did, I would not get angry. He had a beautiful farm. He said, "I'll give you this farm. Would you like it?" I said, "Of course."

He smiled. "Your master told you not to be attached, and yet you are very quick to tie yourself to a farm." I felt very small. My mind seemed bent toward anger and attachment and not toward higher things.

Later I was sent to still another swami. He knew that I was coming. There was a small natural fountain on the way where we used to go and wash. He left some gold coins there. I stopped there and I found three of them. For a second I entertained the thought of picking them up. I did so, and tucked them inside my loincloth. Then I reconsidered: "But these coins are not mine. Why do I need them? This is not good." I put them back.

When I went to the swami, he was annoyed. I bowed before him and he said, "Why did you pick up the coins? Do you still have lust for gold? Get out. This is not the place for you."

I protested, "But I left them there."

He said, "You left them later on. The problem is that you were attracted to them and picked them up in the first place."

From the experiences that these sages gave me I began to realize the difference between book knowledge and experiential knowledge. I began to see my many weaknesses, and I did not find it pleasant. Finally I returned to my master. He asked, "What have you learned?"

"I have learned that I have intellectual knowledge, but I do not behave in accord with that knowledge."

He said, "This is the problem all intellectuals have. They become overly proud of their knowledge. Now I will teach you how to practice, so that you will know."

A human being may know enough, but that knowledge needs to be brought into daily life. If this is not done, the knowledge remains limited. We all know what to do and what not to do, but it is very difficult to learn how to be. Real knowledge is found not in knowing but rather in being.

Practice makes Perfect

Once when I was teaching about life and death, a swami quietly came in and sat with my students. I thought that he was a beginner, so I treated him as I treated the others. I was annoyed because he only smiled, while the others were conscientiously taking notes. I finally asked, "Are you listening to me?"

He said, "You are only talking, but I can demonstrate mastery over life and death. Bring me an ant."

A large ant was brought. He cut it into three pieces and separated them. Then he closed his eyes and sat motionless. After a moment the three parts moved toward each other. They joined together, and the revived ant scurried away. I knew it was not hypnosis, or anything like that.

I felt very small before that swami. And I was embarrassed before my students because I only knew the scriptures without a firsthand understanding and mastery of life and death. I asked, "Where did you learn that?"

He said, "Your master taught me."

At that I became angry with my master and immediately went to him. Seeing me he asked, "What happened? Why are you once again allowing anger to control you? You are still a slave to your violent emotions."

I said, "You teach others things which you don't teach me. Why?"

He looked at me and said, "I have taught you many

things—but you don't practice. That is not my fault! All these achievements depend on practice, not just on verbal knowledge of them. If you know all about the piano but don't practice, you will never create music. Knowing is useless without practice. Knowing is mere information. Practice gives direct experience, which alone is valid knowledge."

The Sage from the Valley of Flowers

There was not much literature on the flowers and ecology of the Himalayas, but whatever was available, I tried my best to go through. After reading a book by a British author about the valleys of flowers, a flame of burning desire arose in my heart. In the Himalayas there are countless varieties of lilies, rhododendrons, and other flowers, but I specifically was anxious to see one of two valleys.

I knew a sage who constantly traveled in the Valley of Flowers region of the Himalayas. He was very strong and healthy and about eighty years of age. He always carried a unique blanket. This blanket weighed approximately eighty to one hundred pounds. You might wonder how he made this blanket so heavy. Any piece of cloth which he found during his travels, he would patch onto the blanket. It was a blanket of a thousand patches. He called it *gudari*, which means "blanket of patches," and people called him Gudari Baba.

In answer to my request to visit the Valley of Flowers he said, "If you would really like to see the Valley of Flowers and want to follow me, you will have to carry this blanket."

I agreed, but when I put the blanket on my shoulders I stumbled under its weight. He asked, "How is it possible for a young man like you to be so weak when you are apparently so healthy?" He picked up the blanket and said, "See how light it is?" Then he put it on my shoulders again. He knew my master and so he allowed me to follow him to the Valley of Flowers.

As I was following him this sage said, "No one can retain his memory when he goes through the Valley of Flowers during the blooming season. We should bring all the obstinate kids like you here and set them right. Those who try to be intellectual and argue with us should be brought here so that they understand their worth."

I said, "But I am following you."

He said, "Oh yes. You argue all the time and don't listen attentively. You are very proud of your intellectual knowledge. I do not know how to read and write. You are more educated than I. You have education, but I have control of mind."

I told him, "I also have control." He replied, "We

shall see."

I said, "Sir, first of all, please take away your blanket from my shoulders because it is difficult to carry." He lamented, "Oh, the children of this modern age!"

He took his blanket from me and started conversing with it: "O my beloved blanket, nobody understands anything about you. No one knows that you are a living blanket." I looked at him and thought, "This man is really crazy!"

The next morning a Japanese monk joined us. He was equally anxious to see the Valley of Flowers. This Japanese monk also thought that Gudari Baba was a crazy man. He asked me, "Rama, can you explain why this man is carrying such a heavy load?" We started talking and I thought it would be nice to share these experiences with each other.

This monk was afraid of going to the Valley of Flowers all alone. Someone had told him that if any traveler goes to see this valley, he forgets everything and his senses do not coordinate in perceiving sense objects. The traveler loses his memory and smiles all the time. He said that this baba was the right person to guide us because he traveled in this region and knew all the trails.

The next day this Japanese monk started shivering with fever. He had lived in the jungles of Burma and had suffered from malaria. He had a temperature of 103 to 104 degrees and his pulse rate was very high. The baba said to him, "You told this boy that I was crazy. Do you want to see the living power of my blanket? Do you know that this blanket is not a mere blanket, but a living force? Do you want to get well? Then kneel down and be humble!" The baba covered the Japanese monk with the blanket.

The monk said, "I will be flattened! It's too heavy and I am a small man."

The baba said, "Keep quiet!" After a few minutes he took the blanket away from the monk. When he removed the blanket, it was shivering. The baba asked the monk, "What happened to your fever?"

He said, "Sir, I don't have a fever anymore."

The baba said, "This blanket is very generous and kind and has taken away your fever." The baba looked at me and said, "Do you want his fever to be cured forever?" I said, "Yes, please."

The baba said, "But he calls me crazy. I don't think

he deserves my help."

I said, "The sages are kind and great and they always forgive others."

The baba smiled and said, "Of course I will help him." We traveled together for fifteen days and the Japanese monk did not suffer from the fever again.

Nine miles outside of Badrinath on a side trail which leads to the Valley of Flowers there is a small *guru dwara* (temple of Sikhs). We took our meal there. We rested that whole day in the temple and started our journey to the Valley of Flowers the next day.

The flowers were in full bloom as far as the eye could see. For the first few hours it was soothing to the senses and stimulating to the

"YOUR EDUCATION AND STRENGTH HAVE NO VALUE FOR THEY DO NOT STAND WITH YOU IN TIME OF NEED."

mind. But slowly I started noticing that my memory was slipping away. After five or six hours the baba asked, "Hey you! Can you tell me your name?"

We were both so disoriented that we could not remember our names. We had completely forgotten them. I was only aware of my existence and had a hazy idea that I was with two other people. That's all. The fragrance of those flowers was so strong that we could not think rationally. Our ability to reason wouldn't function. Our senses were anesthetized. We had a faint idea of our existence and that of the things around us. Our talk to each other did not make any sense. We lived in this valley for a week. It was highly enjoyable. The baba made fun of us all the time and said, "Your education and strength have no value."

After we came out of the Valley of Flowers, the baba said, "Your joy was because of the influence of the fragrance of the flowers. You were not meditating. That's what marijuana and hashish do to people, and they think that they are in meditation. Look at me. I was not affected or influenced by the fragrance of those wild flowers. Ha, ha, ha!

"You have gone to college and have read many books. You have lived on the opinions of others so far. Today you had a good chance to understand and compare direct knowledge and the so-called knowledge which is really imitation. So far the opinions that you have are actually the opinions of others. Those who live on the opinions of others do not ever have the ability to decide and express their own opinions. Boys, this informative knowledge is not considered by us to be real knowledge. Even if you understand that direct knowledge alone is valid, you don't have control over the mind. The education given to modern children is very superficial. Without any discipline, control over the mind is not possible–and without control of the mind, direct experience is impossible."

The Japanese monk left for Bodhi Gaya, and I lived with the baba for another fifteen days. He is a free wanderer of this region, and all the pilgrims have heard about him.

Spiritual Dignity Is Also Vanity

After I had renewed my resolve to follow the path of renunciation, my master thought I was feeling guilty, so he told me to live on a bank of the Narmada River, which flows through central India, and to practice certain austerities there. He instructed me to go to an isolated, dense forest thirty miles south of Kherighat, near Omkareshwar.

The river there was full of crocodiles, and in the mornings and evenings several of them would lie on the sand along the river. I lived on the riverbank for six months without anyone disturbing me. I had only a water pot, a blanket, and two loincloths. People from a village

six miles distant supplied me with milk and whole-wheat bread once a day. Those six months of intense physical and mental austerities were a high period in my life.

One day a party of big-game hunters came by and saw me sitting in meditation on the sand in the midst of many crocodiles, some of whom were lying just a few yards away from me. The hunters took my photograph without my noticing and sent it to a newspaper. Soon stories about me appeared in many newspapers. At that time the Shankaracharya of Karvirpitham, Dr. Kurtkoti, a highly intellectual man and a Sanskrit scholar of high repute, was searching for his successor.

Shankaracharyas are considered to be the spiritual heads of India, and occupy positions analogous to that of the pope in the Christian tradition. Dr. Kurtkoti instructed a few pandits to observe my daily routine from a distance. They stayed in the village at night and watched my activities during the day. They also collected information from others about my life.

After observing me for some time and carefully investigating my background, they approached me and tried to persuade me to consider becoming Shankaracharya. I was taken to Dr. Kurtkoti, and he took a liking to me. Then I went to my master and received his permission to accept the position.

After a ceremony lasting eighteen days I was installed as a successor of Jagat Guru Shankaracharya. I received thousands of telegrams from well-wishers all over the world, including messages from the pope and other spiritual heads. It was a strange experience for me–such a startling contrast to my six months of solitude and silence. I was less than thirty years old and they gave me such a great responsibility.

Dr. Kurtkoti believed in socio-religious reformation, and handed over his files of valuable correspondence with other spiritual and political leaders. I had numerous meetings with various groups and leaders. I had a busy schedule of traveling and lecturing, and when I wasn't so engaged, people would come to see me from morning to evening and ask for my blessings. It became very difficult for me; I had no freedom. I thought, "I don't get any time to meditate and do my practices; I spend my whole day blessing people. This is not good."

I was not at all happy. My conscience said, "You are not meant for this. Leave!" So after two years I simply ran away, without any money in my pocket. One day I had a large mansion to live in and many cars, and the next I had nothing but the clothes I was wearing. Wanting to return to the Himalayas, I boarded the third-class section of a train which was headed where I wanted to go, even though I had no ticket. The people on the train must have wondered whose clothes I had stolen, because I was still wearing the costly garb of Shankaracharya. When the conductor came he forced me to get off at the next station because I had no money and I didn't want to reveal my identity. I had never before committed such a crime as traveling without a ticket. I just bowed my head and got down, saying humbly, "Thank you for not prosecuting me."

The admirers and followers of Shankaracharya did

not at all appreciate my resigning the dignity and prestige of the position. They felt that I was forsaking my responsibilities—but I had not been happy, and I never returned to that place again.

When I came to my master he said, "You have seen how worldly temptations follow a swami; how the world wants to absorb a spiritual person. Now nothing will affect you, because you have experienced positions, institutions, and renunciation. People expect a lot from their spiritual leaders. Do what you can to uplift and enlighten the people—but never forget your path."

Sri Swami Rama

One of the greatest adepts, teachers, writers, and humanitarians of the 20th century, Swami Rama is the founder of the Himalayan Institute. Born in northern India, he was raised from early childhood by a Himalayan sage, Bengali Baba. Under the guidance of his master he traveled from monastery to monastery and studied with a variety of Himalayan saints and sages, including his grandmaster, who lived in a remote region of Tibet. In addition to this intense spiritual training, Swami Rama received higher education in both India and Europe. From 1949 to 1952, he held the prestigious position of Shankaracharya of Karvirpitham in south India. Thereafter, he returned to his master to receive further training at his cave monastery, and in 1969 came to the United States where he founded the Himalayan Institute. His best known work, *Living with the Himalayan Masters,* reveals the many facets of this exceptional adept and demonstrates his embodiment of the living tradition of the East.

THE HIMALAYAN INSTITUTE

GLOBAL HEADQUARTERS (USA)

The main building of the Institute headquarters near Honesdale, Pennsylvania, USA.

FOUNDED IN 1971 BY SWAMI RAMA, the Himalayan Institute has been dedicated to helping people grow physically, mentally, and spiritually by combining the best knowledge of both the East and the West.

Our international headquarters is located on a beautiful 400-acre campus in the rolling hills of the Pocono Mountains of northeastern Pennsylvania, USA. The atmosphere here is one to foster growth, increase inner awareness, and promote calm. Our grounds provide a wonderfully peaceful and healthy setting for our seminars and extended programs. Students from all over the world join us here to attend programs in such diverse areas as hatha yoga, meditation, stress reduction, ayurveda, nutrition, Eastern philosophy, psychology, and other subjects. Whether the programs are for weekend meditation retreats, week-long seminars on spirituality, months-long residential programs, or holistic health services, the attempt here is to provide an environment of gentle inner progress. We invite you to join with us in the ongoing process of personal growth and development.

The Institute is a nonprofit organization. Your membership in the Institute helps to support its programs. Please call or write for information on becoming a member.

PROGRAMS AND SERVICES INCLUDE:

- Himalayan Institute Press
- *Yoga International* magazine
- Seminars and Workshops
- Meditation Retreats
- Yoga Teacher Training
- Self-Transformation Program™
- Residential Programs
- Pancha Karma
- Himalayan Institute Total Health Products and Services
- Spiritual Excursions
- Humanitarian Projects and Community Centers in Africa, India and Mexico

THE HIMALAYAN INSTITUTE PRESS has long been regarded as the resource for holistic living. We publish books that offer practical methods for living harmoniously and achieving inner balance. Our approach addresses the whole person–body, mind and spirit–integrating the latest scientific knowledge with ancient healing and self-development techniques. As such, we offer a wide array of titles on physical and psychological health and well-being, spiritual growth through meditation and other yogic practices, as well as translations of yogic scriptures.